D1464286

Death on a Live Wire

AND

On Stepping from a Sixth-Storey Window

This is Michael Baldwin's third book of poems. As in the previous volumes, the main impulse remains in areas of personal experience which have been broken into by Myth or enlarged by Miracle. This is not a tentative poetry; its themes uncover a vision at once epic and private; and the language, as always in Mr Baldwin's work, is arresting, personal, and true.

Mr Baldwin started to publish poetry when he was twenty. He has also written novels and plays, and has collaborated in a musical. He is married and has two children.

Death on a Live Wire

AND

On Stepping
from a
Sixth-Storey
Window

BY

Michael Baldwin

 LONGMANS

LONGMANS, GREEN AND CO LTD
48 Grosvenor Street, London W1
Railway Crescent, Croydon, Victoria, Australia
Auckland, Kingston (Jamaica), Lahore, Nairobi

LONGMANS SOUTHERN AFRICA (PTY) LTD
Thibault House, Thibault Square, Cape Town
Johannesburg, Salisbury

LONGMANS OF NIGERIA LTD
W. R. Industrial Estate, Ikeja

LONGMANS OF GHANA LTD
Industrial Estate, Ring Road South, Accra

LONGMANS GREEN (FAR EAST) LTD
443 Lockhart Road, Hong Kong

LONGMANS OF MALAYA LTD
44 Jalan Ampang, Kuala Lumpur

ORIENT LONGMANS LTD
Calcutta, Bombay, Madras
Delhi, Hyderabad, Dacca

LONGMANS CANADA LTD
137 Bond Street, Toronto 2

Printed by
Western Printing Services Ltd
Bristol

Contents

DEATH ON A LIVE WIRE

Vibrations 9
A Nest of Epitaphs 10
Seen from Outside 16
Death on a Live Wire 17
Storm 19
Transplanted 21
Speechhouse 22
The Buried God 24
The Bride House 25
Planting a Beast 27
Prayer 28
Trees 29
Piscator 30
Wasdale Head Church, 1957 31
Man with Animals 32
Saint and Demon 33
The Forest of Dean 34
Observation 35
Chalk Horse 36
The Lesson 37
The Three Triads 38
Bandstand Trumpeter 39
People 40
Icarus in Winter 41
Parachutist 42
Floods are not the Flood 43
Objection Overruled 45
Man in the Landscape 46
On the Rotation of Crops 47
On the Mediterranean Coast 48
The Water-butt 49
The Weight of Bone 50
Reflections 51

ON STEPPING FROM A SIXTH-STOREY WINDOW

Yes 57
A Skiffle for God in the City 58
A Planned Tomorrow 59
Sweeter Suburbs 60
News 61
Meat in the Head 62
Two Poems for Teds 63
On stepping from a Sixth-Storey Window 65
There's No Room for God in *My* Trousers 66
Modern Lullaby 67
Middle-earth 68
Practice Seawards 69
The Fall of the Angels: Anglo-Saxon 70
Higher Metaphysics 73
Song 74
Steeple-jack 75
Remaking the Riverside 76
A Set of Randy Shanties 77
Sea-net 81
Fishers at the Back of the Town 82
Voyage of Mirrors 83
Gypsy Song 84
Unoriginal Sin 85
England 86
Just a Handful of Red Meat 87
After the Bang 89
Burial Place 91
Epitaph 93

Death
on a
Live
Wire

For
M.R.B.

Vibrations

Why write in verse, when Smith and Green
Were created by God, quite well, in prose?
What Green can see can be clearly seen,
What Smith sets going goes;

And in their ignorance of all
The tall day could oppress them by
They are both quite well;
We are the ones to cry

When Smith and Green, who do not see
Their boots hold down a corner of the nation,
Take the uneven step of Anarchy
And our world rocks because of their elation.

A Nest of Epitaphs

1

Uncle Artemus
With his great bell blunderbuss
Violated the flying blackbirds,
Salting the sky with lead.
Wherever he went there would be
Some five or six feathers to fall on his head
Or the thundered-off tail of a tree.

2

Uncle Cyclops
Had one eye
To bulge at ankles prinking past.
He had no appetite to chew a thigh
But great slob kisses bumbled from his lips
And flew against the model tits in shops.

3

Uncle Dick
Is dead and done up in his bag
And buried in a shadow dug in morning
Mourned by men with tighter trousers and
    straight legs.
But earth at least is manageable material
And stitched into his last coat by the worms
Dick fits it better daily, with the girls
To weed his whiskers, and his toes
All ending in a salty crop of corms.

4

To be famously buried, the hero's quest:
Here Uncle Tom does rest
In the greenest glade in the forest.
He has gone in melons through the little children,
He sits bluebottled on the end of your nose.

The ocean also will number him,
Swung on the round-shot round
Or kegged in wrecks where the fish
Swim full of doubloons. Eyes wash up on the sand
And feet are cut on his teeth.

Listen now how the waves
Say Icarus. Some came
Back from the dead and had their fame
Only once: Jonah, Lazarus.
The second time no-one knew where they went.

5

Drink up, grandad,
Drool your beer
Over the lowest easiest lip.
Hang up your leer
With the barmaid there,
It's time to kip.

O tell me,
Pivoted on your arse,
Bloodshot eyes, churchwarden stare
And fifty years of unfocused wit,
What metaphysics fill up the glass
When the beer drains out of it.

6

Carving a placid grace
At seasides, ignoring the true salt
Or the navel that winked in the sun
He found how much to efface.

He knew what mastery he had avoided
To make those simpering thighs
They would argue about in the public
  garden
And dawn discover with red paint.

He addressed more imperfect bone
In a model's blanket,
Yet would not own
That life is what has been done
In spite of the artist's lies.

Seen from Outside

There's glass on the churchyard wall
To keep the little children
Out of the field of God;
All night the cut cats call
Redbellied to the stars,
All day the sparrows fall
With splinters in their claws
To ripen in the grass
With Martha, John and Paul
Who lie beneath the wall
Suckers for the laws.

Death on a Live Wire

Treading a field I saw afar
A laughing fellow climbing the cage
That held the grinning tensions of wire,
Alone, and no girl gave him courage.

Up he climbed on the diamond struts,
Diamond cut diamond, till he stood
With the insulators brooding like owls
And all their live wisdom if he would.

I called to him climbing and asked him to say
What thrust him into the singeing sky:
The one word he told me the wind took away,
So I shouted again, but the wind passed me by

And the gust of his answer tore at his coat
And stuck him stark on the lightning's bough;
Humanity screeched in his manacled throat
And he cracked with flame like a figure of straw.

Turning, burning, he dangled black,
A hot sun swallowing at his fork
And shaking embers out of his back,
Planting his shadow of fear in the chalk.

O then he danced an incredible dance
With soot in his sockets, hanging at heels;
Uprooted mandrakes screamed in his loins,
His legs thrashed and lashed like electric eels;

For now he embraced the talent of iron,
The white-hot ore that comes from the hill,
The Word out of which the electrons run,
The snake in the rod and the miracle;

And as he embraced it the girders turned black,
Fused metal wept and great tears ran down
Till his fingers like snails at last came unstuck
And he fell through the cage of the sun.

Storm

I heard the thunder rolling past the window,
I saw the bulging cloud, the glowing post
And the upright grass without air
Waiting for the downpour of space, the field
Bruised by the weight of an acre of wind
Flat beyond the tremble of the window,
And the window waiting wild with light

For the thistle-crack or the cruel crescendo
Of soundless water walking through the trees
From the beat of the wind. I looked at my watch,
It stood at day; need I wonder
At the greenness of objects in artificial dark,
At the invisible crouch of the hill
Beyond the wood, beyond the tree beyond the window?

I turned to myself, the room in electric leaf,
The wireless-set waiting to be tuned to thunder,
So I switched it on. At once came the crash
Of ages discharging their crystal grief,
Of aeons avoiding the tingle of time,
White lines exploded in the screen of day
And darkness tore with its forks at the hills

While electrons renewed their giant embrace
As the thunder-drops grinning with tension passed
And their green light fell and refreshed the grass.
A new sun opened itself in my eye,
And the hill and the hill's edge of sky
Were at peace in the night together, and moved
As they should in the long roll of space.

Transplanted

Persuade me to ignore the town
The red buses and the dead men
Who ride on them, the can
That cuts its teeth on a dog's legs
And the boy in rags
Who digs his fingers down
Through the grating's ribs
Into the heart of it.

This is my day's event:
New towers arise; wheels turn
My belly round like wet cement,
I see the brick fill in
The last cracks of the sun.

This is no pastoral grief; I grieve
For the child who comes
Into this leafless grave
And loves the stone that fosters it,
Till his eyes are stone
And his teeth are stone
And from their henge of stone
Bounces the stone of spit.

Speechhouse

*A monologue by an old miner
now only fit for surface-working,
overheard in the Forest of Dean*

Not so wise, no more words
In my beak. I left my voice
A century ago in the galleries
Underneath Speechhouse;
My veins are branches of coal,
You know my disease.

My lungs folded up their wings
Like a dying bird, and the corpse
Of my youth cries there, in the galleries
Underneath Speechhouse;
I stretch out my hands for its tongue,
I die of a tongueless disease.

Yet to turn is death. To go into dark
Is death; for now no light
Burns in me. I am sick
With the dark inside me. Over my back
I carry a black sack
And, inside, the bones of dead trees.

These I have won as my due
For toiling in the earth's side.
I breathe on the hill black frost
And my words as I talk to you
Are torn like bark from my side
And crack in the wind:

O sing for me, friend.
You know my disease.

The Buried God

The yellow hillside is a buried God.
Binoculars can see
The flowers forming on his brazen thighs,
The roots that gird up the decaying loins,
And find you, in those dandelions,
The snails that were his testicles.

The form disperses underneath the hill
And every daffodil is tinged with iron
As lovers now embrace within the radius
Of his expanding navel: dogs dig up
The shadow of his vague expanding post
And small boys piddle in the soft clay eyes
Where girls pick violets.
                       Those fondled
Crisp metallic curls, the curios
Of his lower ringlets, rigid iron,
Now glisten in the twiddles of the worms,
Though Time, unlike a worm,
Is all tail and no arse, and devotees
Will need defective vision
And the faith to follow me
If we are fully to agree.
It seems the hill has swallowed him
And not a kneecap
Nuzzles in a flint of all his lineaments.
And yet he's nearer than the other god
And wears the vagueness of nobility.

The Bride House

A broken house, where rust and rime
Riddling the russet leave a core
Untouched by weather but chewed by time:
Maggots use stairs; the second floor
Is given to ghosts, and no-one's rector
Will exorcise the sleepy spectre
Or sever the wraith of a dripping tap.
You take the silence slowly, holding
Hand to rail. With fingered lip
You hear the cornered breezes scolding

The broken house. The teeth of clouds
Nudge ridge and rafter, yawn and bite
Like the bloated maggots of apple-wood;
And shrill winds chew the slates all night

And break the house: some sound cement
For the perambulations of the louse
And sexless spectres spare of scent;
Some twenty wishbone rafters bent
Till tenants whispered, 'a breaking house,'
And took down curtains, half aware
That comprehension, growing dank,
Began to creak like a tortured plank
In the broken house, and, human, left.

I last of all, sensing the end
Of corridors that end on air,
Looking and finding that certain stair
My metaphysics understand
In a tawdry twentieth-century way,
Note the deposits of history
That diminish but do not disappear,
The finality of a rubble of stone;
And standing in the departing air
By the handrail to infinity
Strive to leave one brick in Time,
My root, my ruin, and my rhyme.

Planting a Beast

God looks at man and sees him working well
On elastic acres dripping from the hill;
The map expands, unfolded by the plough;
The plum is picked, and dung repays the straw.
New hedgerows bristle in the wet weight of the wind;
With rafters rising on the back of every hand
The landscape grows familiar: a torn tile
Shrieks like a plundered finger-nail;
So bind your branches, prune the wind, repair
The smallest crack in any pane of air,
For through the chinks assurance runs away
And lightnings tear the paper look of day;
Neglect them for a season and you'll find
In every unclipped shadow of the mind
Hemlock and darnel, dead beaks in the wood
Flints to end a furrow, birds in a mood
Of darkness, round eyes in the wing
Watching your ankles thicken
And the beast take root:
Man with the sky in his nostrils
And a hole where he lifts his foot.

Prayer

Beasts touch the sky with horns,
Men with felt hats.
How do beasts pray?
Men's prayers smell of smoke
All rung off pat.

How do beasts pray?
Do we *think*, in church,
While the stones hang
Down from the cloud like a rope
To be rung with song,

Do we think back to horns?
Beasts wise with birds
In our heads and the hanging stones
Do we think back enough
For the beast in our bones?

Our skulls hold the beast,
Yet our prayer is a cow
With cow-pat eyes.
Prayers should be satyrs
And violate paradise.

Trees

Men tailor trees. With ladder-legs
They cut holes in the shade so sky
Sings holes in them; birds cog
And fidget in suspended cages
Made more intricate for song.
The sunset's scratched from trees by cats
Or hangs in scabs till Autumn rages.

We butcher them at root; but when
The bison's trousers were still on
Men clung to trees, and silkworms spun
The sunshine for their eyelashes,
Birds mated in the beard and groin
While archers feathered shafts with song,
And every shadow was a nest of men.

Piscator

He cast with his eye
Upon the water's glass:
Fish rose like flowers
Gaping in a vase,
But they wouldn't bite.

He lashed with his wrist
Upon the water's back:
It cracked, scabbed, scarred
With scales in each crack,
But they wouldn't bite.

Hand, heart, head
He lowered on a hook:
The water turned crystal,
Fish faces looked,
But they wouldn't bite.

He cast from his loin
Fly, line and pin,
Dancing on the stream
Through gob, gill and fin:
The mermaids pulled him in.

Wasdale Head Church, 1957

Here in this country churchyard
The signs are carved to stand:
The land keeps alive the living
And the dead keep alive the land.

Great beasts drop skulls on the mountain,
And there their horns take root:
The headless herds at pasture
Hide grazing necks in fruit.

Man with Animals

I opened the tin
And the butchered steer
Dripped on my hand,
Till I winced at my royal command.
But I licked my hand,
And I wiped my mind
Of the tin-can
And the lardered dead.

For a second I stood;
And the cat watched
And the dog watched
The second I stood in fur
With a feline tilt to my head.

Saint and Demon

I stand in Church, where windows
Drop their different depths of peace
From the sun's single angle;
Their glaring saints
Are tattooed on my shoulder.

All night I lie
Beneath the falling stars
And wear the boughs
The day holds high;
Their forked unprinted men
Moon through the house,
Embroidering the eye.

They tell me Saint and Demon are remote;
And yet, the demons that my fear creates
I own as mine;
And lying in my patterned counterpane
I also praise whoever made the Saint
To give me light from coloured glass and paint.

The Forest of Dean

The forest is full of fires,
Fires where the forest is burning:
The trees are rooted on coal,
And black a yard up the trunk;
The villagers fill their sack
From a hole in the hill;
The live twig breaks with a snap
And the green leaf, veined with black,
Twitches birds of coal
To scrawl in the skies.
I have clasped black-fingernailed hands
And looked into black-rimmed eyes,
And remember a moment's surprise
When a woman took from her wrap
A stone-white child
And bewildered me with its cries.

Observation

Who tore a woman out of Adam's side
And left in man the cavity
Of love unsatisfied
Has taken from this wall,
Crowned by a horse's head
Steeplecock and thistle,
A stone and let it lie;
Through its hole the winds whistle
The cats creep and the wasps fly;
O come come the Council
And shut this howling eye.

Chalk Horse

Men cut their Gods in the hills
The galloping Gods whose hooves
Go flying away in the grass
When the grass moves in the winds.

We walk our shadows astride
Those shimmering flanks at sunset
And ride with their muscled acres
Into revolving dark.

There as we stride away
While the rhythms run wild in our heart
How many words can we say
For the tulips we tune in the clay

Of our graver God, in the Park?

The Lesson

Talking about poetry
My hands wrap themselves in circles:
Only my hands talk,
And my brain rambles.

Talking about poetry
I stand in the schoolroom,
And my fingers snap like chalk
On the slate of gloom.

Talking I hear voices,
Voices come through me,
Rehearse themselves endlessly
Like pressed discs of poetry.

Talking I know listening:
Some eye my tie rung by rung,
Some watch my hands twittering,
Some seem to die in the sun.

The Three Triads

1

The generations nag
At the young man's leg;
Begotten, they crawl
At the old man's heel,
And moving between man and man in a rag
They drive life's aping shadow up the wall.

2

Man shaped like a root,
Torn by birth from his pit,
Must run mad,
Run as mad as a dog,
Till he lies in dirt
And flowers in it.

3

The stone hollows out a pit,
The ball falls, and the foot
Sticks in its own print;
We sink into hills like seas,
All the dead and the doubly dead
And the burning damned,
All sink till we reach the centre
Of man's mythologies.

Bandstand Trumpeter

Give me a pint of water, boys —
I'll blow the glory of the Lord,
I'll crystallise the day and blow
Diamond, icicle and sword;

And music in a swathe of light
Shall rearrange the roaring grass,
The birds shall gutter silently
And movement fossilise in glass;

The ape shall bare its skeleton
And gibber, barrelling the breeze,
While notes as white as pentecost
Singe the silence from the trees;

And notes the cockatoo shall scream
Like silver pencils write the day,
And furry notes like humming-birds
And pebbled notes, and I shall play

Notes that like the sperm of light
Fly to fertilise the void,
Until the silence walks with me
And lives with me, and calls me God.

People

Growing used to a town
I learn the faces:
In the same shop door
The child is always playing
Who will never grow up.

Growing used to a town
I go away and return;
And always it surprises me
How many children
With dirty graces,
Their stockings twisted like plaits
And their plaits coming undone,
Have changed into slender self-conscious
    girls
And how many children remain.

Icarus in Winter

Layers of sky, breaking:
Put down your stone, urchin,
And from the ice
Take your nailed foot;
You walk on the heart aching
Under those frozen ribs
You scar with your boot.

And if you should drown
In that sun
From the cold sky fallen,
Your father who patched up your flesh
From the odd loves at his disposal
Would wander the maze for ever.
Who else would come from his loins at all?

Parachutist

In case the God is there
You say a prayer
And step into his space
And fall in it
A minute
And a half and land
On the bland lap of the earth,
Get up and dust your doubting down
And whore as before.

Floods are not the Flood

A mile from the spreading sea
With the rain falling down
And sap collapsed in the tree
I look upon waterlogged acres
Becoming first grassy waters
Then glass within fencing squares
Then lakes against windows.

I know there is power
In each diamond drop
To unite and engulf the shore
And bury in liquid light
The squares of next year's crop,
And power more
In these falling windows of air
That smash in the streets
Now the glass is falling in sheets.

But the concepts holding us here
Will not let us wash away:
Ten lorries of gravel a day
Plug the hole in the wall
Till the big tides turn
And the gale forces fall.
The tables say
That the tides and the rains each year
Will enlarge for a little the sea,
But workmen are guarding the pier
And children go down from play
To wait for the shore to appear
And stink like a stranded whale.

Objection Overruled

The hill and the wall on the hill
That has stood for centuries
And the scree falling down from the skies
And the cliff with a hooked bill
Chawing the sun
And the heavy shadow hanging
From a swinging wing
And the dog barking by the beck
At a gasping stone
Is all going under (the papers say)
Six singing pylon-wires,
Is all being ruined
By a dove-tailed dam:
The rock spires and the rock choirs
Are going to drive Birmingham.
Smeared with cement
I suppose the valley looks
A little different,
With its twelve twinkling towers,
And I've counted two tins
In the rust-red rocks,
Two new tins;
But see the mist come down
And the snow come down
(Or even dusk come down)
And ask who wins.

Man in the Landscape

In a lowland country
Flat as a plan
It is easy to see
The function of man:
He cuts roofs into the horizon
To vary its senseless line.

But here, in the forest,
Find me a bird in his beard.
The gentle deer run away
From a shadow striding faster
Than the trees can step
Through the spokes of the day.
He walks with a gun
Like its lord and master.

O he's a hero,
We all know well
He can fly in a cloud
And his looks can kill;
And yet I must own
I have once or twice
On a crag alone
Felt the beast in my skull
Panic aloud,
The will overpowered
By a looming hill.

On the Rotation
of Crops

Acres fold upon acres
The plough can never turn back;
We trap the sun in the dirt
And break it up
To burn in the bladed corn.

Next year we're planting root,
Wurzel, turnip, or beet,
But the field will be gone,
Its character all turned under
Another turn of the sun;

And the workers be gone
Who fathered the corn;
The green, the gold, and the brown
Moving round a place
Put a deeper frown on the face.

The country gives man nothing
But a sense of loss,
His sharpest sense;
How the corn will seem
A year hence

With the back bent on a hoe
And the dirt brown
Between hedgerow and hedgerow.
Man looks back to noble things;
So does a scarecrow.

On the Mediterranean Coast

The crane took a ten-ton stone,
A chipped-off chunk of God,
And dropped it, round and plumb,
In the hole in the harbour wall,
To plug the sea's wail.

I looked inland and saw
The ten-ton hole
Raw in a face of granite
Where they banged it out with a drill:
To succour the crumbling shore,
With its sticks and old tin-cans
And beggars with itching skins,
Is it worth knocking down a hill?
And how many mountains more
Will end in the shunting sea?

The Water-butt

The fact
That a drop
Of water
Throws shadow
Or, rather,
A focus
Of dark on a wall
In its fall
Is enough for terror:

That solids prevent the sun
Is well known; and that
Oceans will swallow the light
In a glue of water,
And that, at ten fathoms,
It's eyeball thick,
And ten-thousand muscles the bone
From a whale's back
You can learn at school.

But sit and watch water fall
From an old spout,
Clean water caught from the sky,
And watch it dispersing the light –

You can see what the rain could do
With a reason why.

The Weight of Bone

O little man, your striding makes
The same shy shadow with the sun
As other men's; do you perceive its thinness,
See that the one dry leaf it rests upon
Is not crushed by its weight
And that the sun, whose loss
Means much to leaves,
Can also put your shadow out
And all its aching bone?
Now that the roaring skies can shout
The little man in all of us
Walks lonely through the town.

Reflections

1

Here in the angled lake,
The fathoms fall fluid from perch,
Eluding the pin on the line
The cat on the willows
The bird who hovers
Over the shallows.

It is too large a lake
To lift with a pin.
No swimmer deepens it much
Or fidgets a fin, and the summers
Suck up no more
Than the sky gave before.

Lift up your fish
And the mystery drips from it
Back to the lake
Which mourns no flesh;
To tear out its heart
Leaves no hole in it.

2

To lift what from the lake with line?
The water's quietness
The bone that swims in liquidness
The shine
Of the slowly swimming sun
That traverses the liquidness
And is the quietness?

Hooks draw a meniscus,
Drop a drop
Jagging the water's scaly lip
But fish
Swim in a light that bends
The rod and rush. O drop
Temptation to their lip

And lift up on a snare of twine
Their quietness.

3

It will not hold you
Or retain the stars
That drown to verify the laws
That find them deeper than this glass
That shows them us.

Yet would you say
You ever put it by,
The mouthless lake
That takes your fly?
Who ever shook the water from his eye?

4

Flesh in the water's eye
Above flexing muscles of stone,
What is your true depth?
Water bends
And the mind bends
And the nature of light is shown

By the string
That could draw you into my hand;
Yet would you be
The same limpid shadow on land
If I pulled you clear?

Your image would break
                        on that bend
And my pin would tear
A hole in your element;
Nor could six yards of string
Show your distance from man.

What is your depth?
Is it peace?

On
Stepping
from a
Sixth-
Storey
Window

For
Max Baldwin

Yes

A sort of average modern man
With pinstripe trousers in a drawer
Imported seedcorn in a can,
I know the rich are poor
And the poor are nearly poor.
When I said Flog the Wog
I meant Flog the Wog,
I'm that sort of pedigree dog:
I'll stand by all the slogans
That make me what I am,
You need guts to be Top Fly
In anybody's jam.
Of course I'd skin my wife, sir,
Or anybody's wife —
I'm not afraid of principles
That cut you like a knife;
I'd rather kill in error
Or terror or in beer
Than walk behind a banner
And lay an easy tear.

A Skiffle for God in the City

I've got a message, the Preacher said,
I've got a message for *you*:
Although it took lots of years to build
This whole damned town is stood on a field;
You can see the grass grow through
You can see the grass grow through.

I've got a message, the Preacher said,
I've got a message for *you*:
Your whole damned body is made of dirt,
If you drop your trousers and lift your shirt
You can see the grass grow through
You can see the grass grow through.

I'm a man, I'm a man, the Preacher said,
As a *man* I speak to *you*!
Then his whole damned sermon blew up and bust
And fell on the town in a heap of dust
You can see the grass grow through
You can see the grass grow through.

A Planned Tomorrow

Along came a thinker, with his glasses full of stars,
His kneecaps round and polished and his penis in a
   vase:
'Bite off your fingers, unplug your pumping heart,
The future needs your brains, my boy, we'll all be in
   the cart!'
I saw his eyeballs splinter and their crystal atoms flash,
His lenses rolled before me in a waterfall of ash.

Along came a poet, with his art upon his sleeve,
A naked woman on his tie, a worm between his teeth:
'Button up your lip,' he cried; 'Chop off your bloody
   head!
The heart must rule tomorrow, or we'll all be dead.'
I saw his sonnet sequences go galloping through Time
And chasing from the rainbows all the birds that
   couldn't rhyme.

Along came a stevedore, with fifteen kids in tow —
Fifteen times the sum of all the father doesn't know:
'The Future is not ruled,' he said, 'by men with heads
   nor hearts,
Posterity is ruled, my boy, by men with private parts!'
I saw the world unwinding like a tattered ball of wool,
And the Ape pick up his spanner, and the Monkey run
   from School.

Sweeter Suburbs

They practise premarital precaution in
The sweeter suburbs. Sex keeps the rule,
A smoky Siamese kitten on its chain.
The trees, like pins stuck in an old maid's wool,
Hide nothing that the rector can't explain.
The rain's one cuspidor is called the Central
    Pool.

And silent children by this vast spittoon
Watch the green water dribble from the tongues
Of unerotic Fauns that will not nod.
Their fathers in the pump-rooms of the town
Deplore the gaunt and razor-tailored young
In trousers with no pocket-room for God.

News

We hired three flat-chested girls
To walk with severed heads in their
    brassieres
To the precinct of St. Paul's:
No-one had noticed them before;
Now there were catcalls,
Offices wailed with desire.

O my lust lust lust
Said a red and yellow red and yellow
    placard
I'll have you or bust,
And a paper-boy eating mustard
Ran his hot tongue round the lot
And fathered a bastard.

They walked past a man who held
Folded beneath his arm the six open
    graves
Price tuppence in News of Our
    World:
They would make good wives
He said with a plum,
And his anger cooled.

Meat in the Head

This is the story of a statue
With an open mouth, catching flies.
Only, being a giant in granite, facing south,
It caught a bird coming back from the Equator
With a bellyful of eggs, and grew wise;
The whistle in its head
Twitted tramps in the park who wore paper
And lovers stuck together like stamps,
And sometimes at dusk in warmer weather
People came to watch
The words fly into its ear
And the thoughts leap from its eyes
And the darting tail of its tongue.
I made a tape of the statue's song
That will last for centuries
On the magnet of a recorder,
And bring me the myth of the uttering stone;
Yet hearing its tinsel chat
I remember and try to forget
Like a childhood dream
How the tongue of a giant
Was clawed out and eaten
By a black cat.

Two Poems for Teds

1

MIXED GROUP

Their thighs gossip of love,
But their smiles hang like stone
From their hair, and their features
Like sculpture cool in the stone.

If I lived with these faces,
The mouths without lips,
The cheeks without blood, I would take
Something sharp and cut
As they cut, words in the wall of man.
As I cut my man I would open
Lips for the words to run,
I would see, congealed on the stone,
Creation, and live, and be done.

2

A VOICE

I was not born of woman, mister.
They mixed me up in the cement mixer,
A fitting for the ten floor flats;
I'm a stone man. Tap my chest,
Watch my spit bounce.
I speak with a gravel mouth
And drip like a tap.

Don't you like what I say?
Stand aside: that's my part of the sun
And my acre of stone;
You can keep all it's standing on,
All the dead corn,
And the dickie-birds down in the drain.

On Stepping from a Sixth-Storey Window

'Jump then, Jump!
You will hit the pavement at 32 ft. per sec. squared
Minus drag and the wind expelled from your guts
With a bloody awful thump.
And your ankles will telescope into your knees
And your shin-bones run up your thigh
And your thigh-bones remain undigested
In your abdomen till they bury you
In a short coffin!'

'You've got me scared.'

'I don't know why you should be scared, honey.
You'll be dead within five seconds of leaving
This sixth-storey window. Think about me! —
I've got to walk down six flights of stairs
To a bloodstained log
And identify you. *Identify you!*
I didn't marry anyone looking like that.
Good-bye, honey.'

There's No Room for God in My Trousers

All right, Deity, let's agree
That by your standards I'm no good.
I've read that book of yours
But I'm not in the mood for God —
Have you made a film I can see?

Tell me this: is there anything,
I don't care what, but anything you can do
Rather well, like sing
Or rock-'n'-roll or screw,
Or *anything* I can grasp as you?

Is there? If there's *anything*,
Man to man, we'll be there
Making your plateful of sixpences ring,
And no-one'll stop us —
Not you — nor the Coppers.

Modern Lullaby

Lysol for the Devil
That gargles down the drain,
An aerial for the Angel on the tiles,
While the man inbetween
Loves the woman inbetween
And smiles and smiles and smiles.

Power from the pylon
That bumbles down the lane
And lights all the stars at night,
O Good God
We don't need a God
Now we've got the electric light!

Rats within the rafters,
Birds inside the pane,
The scarecrow grins on its stick,
But stick a brick
On top of a brick
And the brick and the brick will stick.

Lysol for the Devil
That gargles down the drain,
An aerial for the Angel on the tiles,
While the man inbetween
Loves the woman inbetween
And smiles and smiles and smiles.

Middle-earth

Men without Heaven or Hell,
Condemned to roam
Between brick and iron,
All night going upstairs to pray,
All day on the level to moan
While Nick chuckles down in the drain:

Come let us ring on this bell,
Fire off this Bomb or Gun,
Till the stormclouds like elephants kneel
And The Big Fellow chucks us a bun —
Which we needn't pick up, just for fun.

Each little bird has its tree,
Each little dog has its bone;
Each little bloke's got his bed and his coat,
And snug in each city of stone
Is the button that sends up the sun.

Practice Seawards

Tomorrow moon the soldiers march
Through the big arch
Down to the gun.
They push cotton fingers into their ears
Then rattle the moonlight all over the town.

The monotonous sea, a motionless whale
Harpooned by shell,
Suddenly spouts,
Then massages wounds with its usual roll
While the gun's deaf soldiers turn sharp
   about

And, yawning cordite, proudly march
Back through the arch
Away from the gun,
Teeth oozing spittle like a cracked cup,
Eardrums fermenting the echoing stone.

At last, all aching ribs ceasing to rattle,
Townspeople settle.
Chivvied by fishes
Already the sunken missile dissolves.
All praise to the monster's digestive juices.

The Fall of the Angels:
Anglo-Saxon

Defenestrated, Satan fell
Head over hills, holding a pint of shandy
And a blond ankle, while he bounced
Down the corny cobbles of the stars.
The Lord stood bailiff on the stairs
And the assistant evictors wiped their
   whiskers
And stood there spoiling for a fight
And hoping they'd won.
           Satan was holding in his hand
A testicle belonging to an Angel,
A Good Angel who knew he'd have to be
A Very Good Angel from now on.
Satan was hoping to give it back to him
If he saw him; but upstairs and downstairs
It was the end of the fun.

How happy we all were, Mrs Sim, and Sam,
And the others at Seventy-Two
And across the road at Seventy-Three,
When they put out Syd
Lock, stock,
And stinking Barrel
Into the street. And Mr Jackson,
Nice Mr Jackson who took the place,
Said it made him sick, *and* his wife,
Just mopping it up, while bottles
Popped their corks with a rude noise
(And him used to blowing bass
In the Salvation Army Band!)
They wouldn't put the Nipper
Where Syd used to sleep with his mandolin
(And he really did, I saw it
Wrapped on his pillow in his shirt –
He loved his music like a wife,
Such dirty music,
But he loved it.)

And Mr Jackson loves music too,
Nicer music, and so does his wife,
And they never blew a false note,
Only once, when they slept out of turn
And now here's Nipper playing on his flute.

And when I think of God I remember
    Mr Jackson
Tucked up tight in my prayers.

It's all right, boys, said Satan,
The Cops don't patrol this side the Canal,
It'll do us fine, this slag-tip
Of the Divine Cosmography:
Better to drink in Hell
Than serve the drinks in Heaven;
Hoboing suits me swell;
They can't be having much fun
Up There, without *us* to kick around –
I guess we've won;

Goodness needs someone to spit on . . .

Nice Mr Jackson!

Higher Metaphysics

The balloon has gone up
And the 'chute descended:
One
Like a bubble of wind in the guts
Pushing upwards under the heart,
The other, a plunge into seven hundred
Feet of metaphysics, a spiral
Of starlings, and one or two people
Eyeing us in anticipation of failure.

Nor in the end are we wiser
By being thirty seconds afraid.
Merely older.

Song

I went out with the little girl in scarlet;
She took it off, and with her yellow frock
I danced a slow gavotte
And spun her through the subtleties of lilac.

Alone at last upon a cold verandah
I felt beneath the yellow to the pink.
She touched an empty eyelid with her finger,
The eye my hand encountered did not blink.

A kiss or two, and she replaced the yellow;
A dance or two, and she replaced the red;
A walk or two, and she was my bedfellow
And all she was lay folded by the bed.

Steeple-jack

I saw the jack lean outward into space
And scrub the steeple with a handful of fresh air.
Was it a halo or a human face
So far above our hundred-headed stare?

I looked around: A Mrs Smith,
The local gawk, deserting from her queue,
Breathed onions at my elbow; and a youth
(The Press) fidgeted for a snap or two.

Suppose he fell! We tasted the event,
Tearing his hands and knees against the wall,
Then burst him brainless on the sharp cement;
Nobody knew him. Yes, suppose he fell:

The pictures lean out grinning from the page –
A spider, broken from his chain of air,
The blurring fall, and then this soggy smudge,
And *me*, in headlines, *Punctually There!*

And yet, of course, it was the House of God;
There might be some protection for these men:
He might float down, or catch upon a cloud –
Who would believe a simple snapshot then?

Remaking the Riverside

They're pulling down the town
The original town,
And planting tulips
To tidy the banks of time.

The Council said it should go
The Sixteenth Century that smelled of God;
Now the gasworks glow
Down a clean road.

But the sky will not recover
Those rickety mislaid roofs,
Nor the town be the same by the river
With no shadow to drag in the mud.

A Set of Randy Shanties

1

Randy on a shandy
   And half-a-pint of port
Jane let her lover
   Do more than he ought:

Deep down inside her
   The dolphins roar and play,
While he's in his lighthouse
   Across the bright blue bay.

2

Jug and Bottle, Jug and Bottle,
Waves suck pebbles on the shore
And spit on sands a dirty dottle,
Fishwives gossip by the door;

Can and candle, Can and candle,
Fishwives gossip by the door
And spit a pint of dirty scandal,
Waves suck pebbles on the shore;

Jug and candle, can and Bottle,
Old men loll upon the shore
And spit on sands a dirty dottle,
Sow the waves with hooks and snore.

3

Pretty on the pier
Wet with a pint of beer,
Round with a rising gust
Ripe as the Holy Ghost,
No kings or kingdoms come
At your bed-post
And the star that hovered here
Has gone past:
I see it sailing seaward
Nailed to a trawler's mast.

4

Suppose the waves discover
Daisy's got a lover!
Will they rise and roar
Or whisper as before?

O the waves too are ripe
With the dark deeds of fish
And learn to bite their lip
When anybody's rash.

Let the shingle cover
Daisy and her lover:
The thrusting sea and shore
Obey no moral law.

Sea-net

There goes many a sailor
Drinking up old tar,
With veins as dark as cord
And muscles pickled hard.

Children haunt their loin
Like shrimps about a corpse;
A hundred bottled brides
Wave to a hundred ships,

And long afloat they weave
The will of those wives
Into the miles of net
That drag the drowned to port.

Fishers at the Back of the Town

High overhead the sun
Chokes with the cinders of dead birds
And the feathers blown
From factory furnaces all over town;
The trees stand like tanneries
Browning their yellow leaves
On the winds of Autumn;
Women of suet stand
For time without end.

So the men sit down
Here at the pool by the town
Where the town began
And fish their face in the water.
They drop their line through the sun
To draw back a cork of stone
From which mud-branches rise.
One hooks a long-dead bird
And one his own drowning eyes.

Voyage of Mirrors

Under the crane's great flail
The ribs of ships in cold harbour
Lie torn and pale;
They turn from the shunting trains
That duplicate in water,
To drop bright hooks and chains
Through the storeyed glass of the bay.

Shyly their bitten keels
Hide in the deepening water
Each eyeshade barnacle,
Then as their wakes congeal
On the flat mud of the harbour
Move to unbroken seas
Where fishes mock monsters from their
    depth of peace.

Gypsy Song

Acorns, the good oak's testicles,
The conker in its curls,
Spill on this servile country
The branch that breaks the hills.

I hear the blackbird calling
Out of the butcher's hair,
The wild green shades of morning
Follow me to the fair.

Unoriginal Sin

In the beginning was the word
That said that men must kiss and tell:
Adam was true to Paradise,
But true to Eve as well.

So out he went, his wits in fig,
To walk the world on broken feet.
Love, for the things that Adam did,
I bless him every time we meet.

England

The acorn struck, the oak
Came up against the sun;
The sower planted shock
On shock of grizzled corn
And the procreant hoof paced on.

Building, boat, and plane
Out of that first royal root
Rose to the help of man:
I look down at a foot
Kicking an old tin can.

Just a Handful of Red Meat

Two ghosts rose up early
Out of the bearded rye,
Said one to the other
Never say die!

*Though we are dead already
And they say the world is dead
No matter how dead the world is
The world is life*, he said

*And the world shall be my woman
Just a handful of red meat,
I'll serve her till damnations
Cry dangling from her teat*

*And she can souse and suckle
The devils with pink gin,
Her lipstick kiss can scratch me
As red as any pin*

*And she can be unfaithful,
Infidelities are true,
O any sin were welcome
To the likes of me and you:*

*We'll kick the saints and sinners
Out of the holy grove
And needle lonely virgins
From grave and grief and groove.*

They walked on together
Between the long-legged trees
And leered at the threadbare birches
That lifted in the breeze;

Just a handful of red meat, they said
A handful of red meat!
Then the world blew asunder
And its good blood splashed their feet.

After the Bang

We came back to the city
In ones and twos and threes,
And some in halves and quarters
And some upon their knees.

With a compass and a geiger
We moved on powdered stone
Where the gelatine archangels
Sucked their drying chips of bone:

The centre of the city
Was storeys deep in death,
The geiger chirruped gently
And the broken held their breath;

We turned back through the suburbs
Where meat dripped in the trees
And breasts like old bananas
Hung peeling in the breeze

And eyeballs rolled like marbles
Along the glass-strewn floor
And the rats came out and sniffed them
And let them roll some more.

Farther out the schoolgirls
Lay frying in their fat
And the dead skull was drying
Inside its cinder hat;

We lingered where the steeple
Had raped the crowded bus,
The world seemed full of flies there
And the flies seemed full of us:

Let's cobble the new city
With the kneecaps of the damned
And call, God Queen & Country
When the next last war is planned.

Burial Place

I walked within the precincts of St. Michael & All
   Souls,
The burial place of all my local saints,
The farmer crucified on waggon-wheels,
The witches boxed in cinder, and the girls
Still simmering in silk beside
The choirboys pickled in their broth of bells.

The knotted worms
That are the world's intestines
Swallowing the dark
Retched up a portion of St. John and said
The words we've heard are wind,
The lips we've listened to are turds
Like any curly one;
O we have striven hard
To liberate the bone,
That edifice of light.

I saw old women weeping on the chalk,
And then the bonehouse feathers blow and walk;
The bird became a skeleton of galvanised desire:
I watched one pull a worm or snap a stalk
And then the tidy women disappear;
And then my buried griefs began to talk:
O you must learn to bear
Your grinning skull of light
And what green fruit lies there.

And still I heard the words within the wind,
And voices hang in silence then take flight;
I lifted up a pencil and now write
These words; but notice how a stone
That grief has carved upon
Stands simple and unuttered while I write.

Epitaph

Summer came low and the sun erupted
And printed mankind on a stone:
Now the Man-Child tires of affection
And the three-headed women groan.